■SCHOLAST

File-Folder Games *in COLOR*

Time & Money

by Immacula A. Rhodes

New York • Toronto • London • Auckland • Sydney
Mexico City • New Delhi • Hong Kong • Buenos Aires

Teaching *Resources*

With love to Doreen and Danelle, and in memory of Dustin

"He has made everything beautiful in its time. He has also set eternity in the hearts
of men; yet they cannot fathom what God has done from beginning to end."

—Ecclesiastes 3:11

Cover and interior design by Jason Robinson
Cover and interior illustrations by Rusty Fletcher

ISBN-13: 978-0-545-22607-3

Text copyright © 2010 by Immacula A. Rhodes
Illustrations copyright © 2010 by Scholastic Inc.
Published by Scholastic Inc. All rights reserved.
Printed in China

2 3 4 5 6 7 8 9 10   16 15 14 13 12 11 10

Contents

File-Folder Games

About This Book

File-Folder Games in Color: Time & Money offers an engaging and fun way to motivate children of all learning styles and help build their knowledge of time and money concepts. Research shows that activities such as games encourage children to communicate their thinking and clarify and organize information. In addition, the games in this book will help children meet important math standards. (See What the Research Says and Meeting the Math Standards, page 6, for more.)

The games are a snap to set up and store: Just tear out the full-color game boards from this book, glue them inside file folders, and you've got ten instant learning center activities. Children will have fun as they match digital times to time phrases in Perfect Pooch Academy, practice different units of time in Time Tiger, match coins to their values in Money Merry-Go-Round, find the value of coin combinations in Build the Bank, and much more.

What's Inside

Each game includes the following:

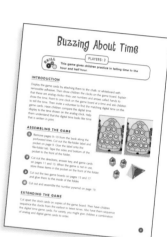

- an introductory page for the teacher that provides suggestions for introducing the game

- step-by-step assembly directions

- Extending the Game activities to continue reinforcing children's skills and interest

- a label with the title of each game for the file-folder tab

- a pocket to attach to the front of the file folder for storing the game parts

- directions that explain to children how to play the game

- an answer key

- game cards

- one or more game boards

- some games also include game markers and a game cube, number pyramid, or spinner

Making the File-Folder Games

In addition to the game pages, you will need the following:

- 10 file folders (in a variety of colors, if possible)
- scissors
- clear packing tape
- glue stick or rubber cement
- paper clips
- brass fasteners

Tips

- Back the spinners, game cubes, number pyramids, and game markers with tagboard before assembling. Laminate for durability.
- Before cutting apart the game cards, make additional copies (in color or black and white) for use with the Extending the Game activities.
- Place the accessories for each game, such as spinners, game cubes, number pyramids, and game markers, in separate, labeled zipper storage bags. Keep the bags in a basket near the games.

Using the File-Folder Games

- Before introducing the games to children, conduct mini-lessons to review the time and money concepts used in each game.
- Model how to play each game. You might also play it with children the first time.
- Give children suggestions on how to determine the order in which players take turns, such as rolling a die and taking turns in numerical order.
- Store the games in a math center and encourage children to play in pairs or small groups before or after school, during free-choice time, or when they have finished other tasks.
- Send the games home for children to play with family members and friends.
- Use the Extending the Game activities to continue reinforcing children's skills and interest.

Storage Ideas

Keep the file-folder games in any of these places:

- math center
- vertical file tray
- file box
- file cabinet
- bookshelf
- plastic stacking crate

What the Research Says

Research shows that activities in which children can communicate their thinking helps to deepen their understanding of mathematical concepts. While playing a math game, for example, players might challenge each other's answers. "Students who are involved in discussions in which they justify solutions—especially in the face of disagreement—will gain better mathematical understanding as they work to convince their peers about differing points of view" (Hatano & Inagaki, 1991, as cited in *Principles and Standards for School Mathematics,* 2000).

Meeting the Math Standards

Connections to the McREL Math Standards

Mid-continent Research for Education and Learning (McREL), a nationally recognized nonprofit organization, has compiled and evaluated national and state curriculum standards—and proposed what teachers should provide for their K–2 students to grow proficient in math, among other curriculum areas. The games and activities in this book support the following standards.

Uses a variety of strategies in the problem-solving process

- Uses discussions with others to understand problems
- Explains how she or he went about solving a numerical problem

Understands and applies basic and advanced properties of the concepts of numbers

- Understands symbolic, concrete, and pictorial representations of numbers
- Understands basic whole number relationships (for example, 4 is less than 10)
- Understands the concept of a unit and its subdivision into equal parts

Understands and applies basic properties of the concepts of measurement

- Understands the concept of time and how it is measured
- Knows procedures for telling time and counting money
- Makes quantitative estimates of familiar time intervals and checks them against measurements

Source: Kendall, J. S., & Marzano, R. J. (2004). *Content knowledge: A compendium of standards and benchmarks for K–12 education.* Aurora, CO: Mid-continent Research for Education and Learning. Online database: www.mcrel.org/standards-benchmarks

Connections to the NCTM Math Standards

The activities in this book are also designed to support you in meeting the following K–2 standards—including process standards, such as problem solving, reasoning and proof, and communication—recommended by the National Council of Teachers of Mathematics (NCTM).

Number and Operations

Understand numbers, ways of representing numbers, relationships among numbers, and number systems

- Connect number words and numerals to the quantities they represent, using various physical models and representations

Understand meanings of operations and how they relate to one another

- Understand the effects of adding and subtracting whole numbers
- Develop and use strategies for whole-number computations, with a focus on addition and subtraction

Measurement

Understand measurable attributes of objects and the units, systems, and processes of measurement

- Recognize the attributes of time
- Compare and order objects according to these attributes

Apply appropriate techniques, tools, and formulas to determine measurements

- Use tools to measure
- Develop common referents for measures to make comparisons and estimates

Source: National Council of Teachers of Mathematics. (2000). *Principles and standards for school mathematics.* Reston, VA: NCTM. www.nctm.org

Buzzing About Time

PLAYERS: 2

 SKILL This game gives children practice in telling time to the hour and half hour.

INTRODUCTION

Display the game cards by attaching them to the chalk- or whiteboard with removable adhesive. Then show children the clocks on the game board. Explain that these are analog clocks—they use numbers and arrows called hands to show the time. Point to one clock on the game board at a time and ask children to tell the time. Then invite a volunteer to find the matching digital time on the game cards. Have children compare the digital time display to the time shown on the analog clock. Help them understand that the digital time looks like time that is written in print.

ASSEMBLING THE GAME

1 Remove pages 9–19 from the book along the perforated lines. Cut out the file-folder label and pocket on page 9. Glue the label onto the file-folder tab. Tape the sides and bottom of the pocket to the front of the folder.

2 Cut out the directions, answer key, and game cards on pages 11 and 13. When the game is not in use, store these items in the pocket on the front of the folder.

3 Cut out the two game boards on pages 15 and 17 and glue them to the inside of the folder.

4 Cut out and assemble the number pyramid on page 19.

EXTENDING THE GAME

Cut apart the clock cards on copies of the game board. Then have children sequence the clocks from the earliest to latest times. Also have them sequence the digital time game cards. For variety, you might give children a combination of analog and digital game cards to order.

Buzzing About Time

Buzzing About Time

GET READY TO PLAY

- Each player chooses a game board.
- Shuffle the cards. Stack them facedown.

TO PLAY

1 Roll the number pyramid. Take that number of cards.
If the pyramid lands on the 🐝, take one card.
Then roll again and take that number of cards.

2 Look at the time on each card. Is that time on a clock on your beehive?
- If so, place the card on the matching clock.
- If not, put the card at the bottom of the stack.

3 After each turn, check the answer key. Is each answer correct?
If not, put that card at the bottom of the stack.

4 Keep taking turns. Try to cover all of your clocks.
The first player to do this wins the game.

Buzzing About Time

ANSWER KEY

Game Board 1	Game Board 2
12:30	12:00
2:00	1:30
2:30	3:00
4:00	4:30
5:30	5:00
6:00	6:30
7:30	7:00
8:00	8:30
9:30	10:00
11:00	11:30

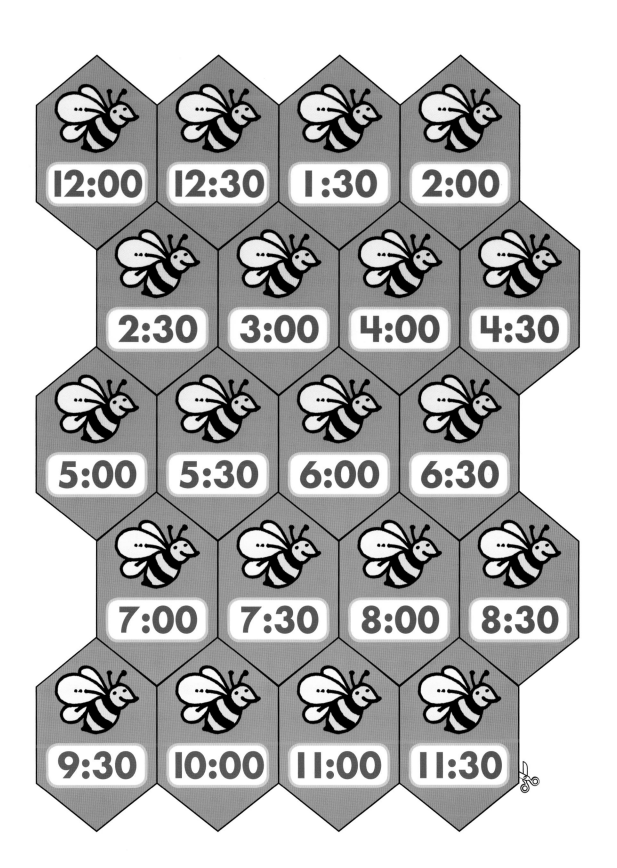

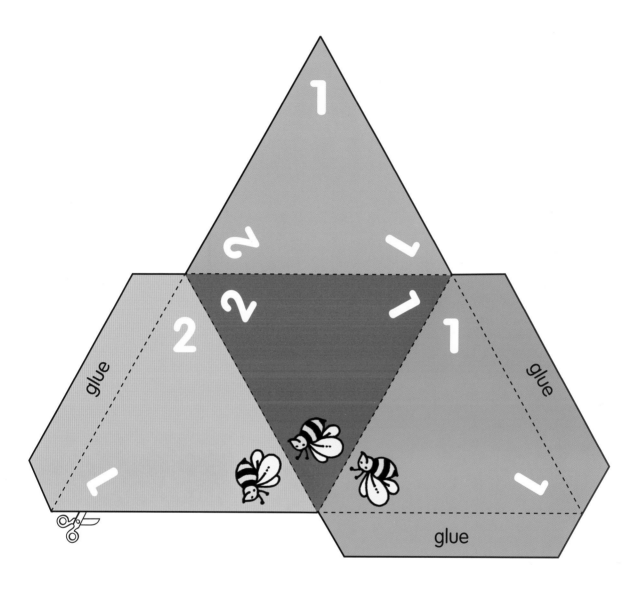

Assemble the pyramid by folding as shown. Glue closed.

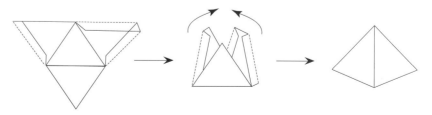

'Round-the-Clock Robots

PLAYERS: 2

 SKILL This game gives children practice in telling time in 15-minute increments.

INTRODUCTION

Display a class clock with movable hands. Show one game card at a time to children. Ask them to name the time shown on the card. Then set the clock to match the time on the card. After demonstrating how to set the clock several times, invite volunteers to set the clock to match the time cards.

ASSEMBLING THE GAME

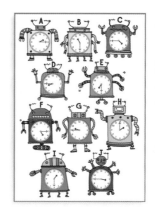

1. Remove pages 23–33 from the book along the perforated lines. Cut out the file-folder label and pocket on page 23. Glue the label onto the file-folder tab. Tape the sides and bottom of the pocket to the front of the folder.

2. Cut out the directions, answer key, and game cards on pages 25 and 27. When the game is not in use, store these items in the pocket on the front of the folder.

3. Cut out the two game boards on pages 29 and 31 and glue them to the inside of the folder.

4. Cut out and assemble the game cube on page 33.

EXTENDING THE GAME

Ask each of two children to choose a game board and then spread the cards facedown on the table. Tell them that, on a signal, they will quickly flip over one card at a time, trying to match the digital times to the clocks on their robots. Each time they find a match, they cover the corresponding robot with the card. If a card is not a match, they return it facedown to the table. The first child to cover all of his or her robots wins the game.

'Round-the-Clock Robots

GET READY TO PLAY

- Each player chooses a game board.
- Shuffle the cards. Stack them facedown.

TO PLAY

1 Roll the game cube. Take that number of cards.
If the cube lands on the , your turn ends.

2 Look at the clock on each card.
Does the time match the time on one of your robots?
  - If so, place the card on that robot.
    - If not, put the card at the bottom of the stack.

3 After each turn, check the answer key. Is each answer correct?
If not, put that card at the bottom of the stack.

4 Keep taking turns. Try to cover all of your robots.
The first player to do this wins the game.

'Round-the-Clock Robots

ANSWER KEY

Game Board 1		**Game Board 2**	
A	2:15	K	3:30
B	11:30	L	12:45
C	4:45	M	5:00
D	8:45	N	9:15
E	7:30	O	6:45
F	5:15	P	6:15
G	9:45	Q	10:15
H	2:00	R	4:30
I	1:30	S	11:00
J	3:45	T	12:15

2:15	3:30	4:45	5:00
6:45	7:30	9:45	10:15
11:00	12:15	1:30	2:00
3:45	4:30	5:15	6:15
8:45	9:15	11:30	12:45

Glue this page to the left side of the file folder.

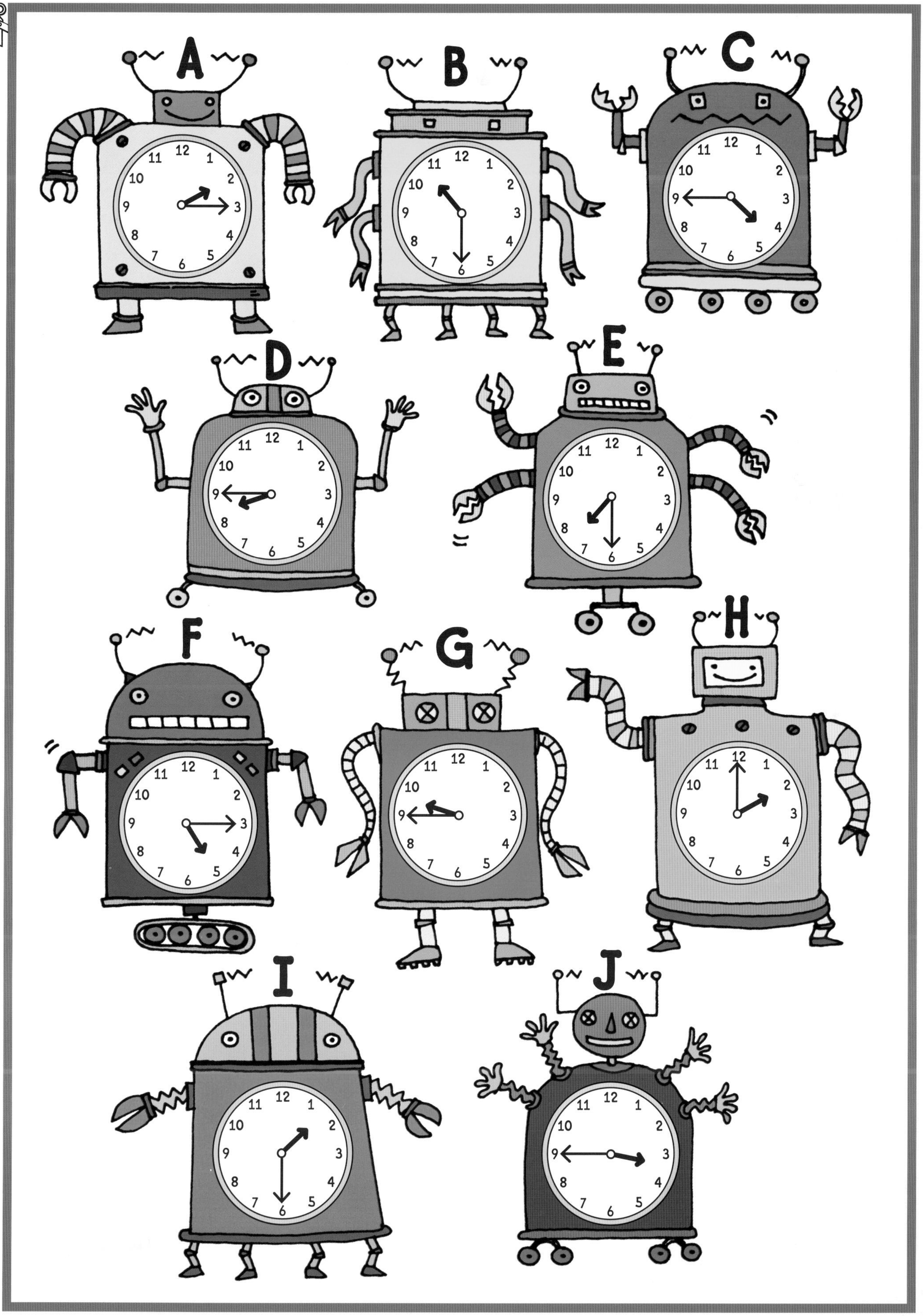

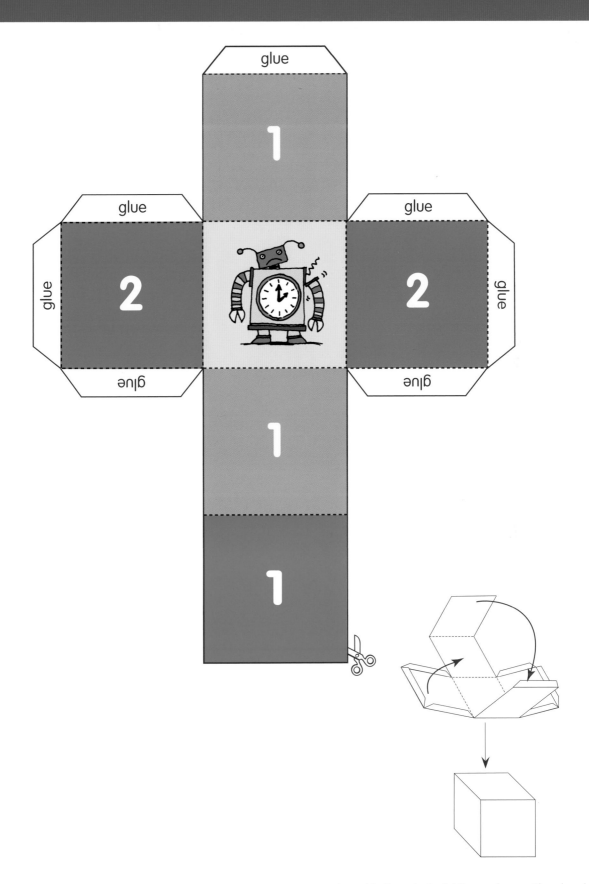

Assemble the cube by folding as shown. Glue closed.

Run Up the Clock

SKILL This game gives children practice in adding time in 10-minute, 30-minute, and one-hour increments.

INTRODUCTION

Set a clock with movable hands to 12:00. Show the clock to children and have them tell the time. Then ask them to tell what time the clock would show if they added 10 minutes to it. Invite a volunteer to set the clock to the new time. Next, reset the clock to 12:00 and have children add 30 minutes, then one hour to the time. Each time, have a child show the new time on the clock. Repeat the activity, using different starting times and having children set the clock 10 minutes, 30 minutes, and one hour later.

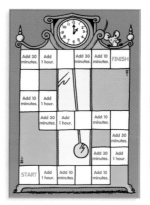
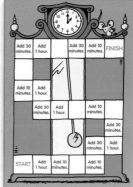

ASSEMBLING THE GAME

1 Remove pages 37–47 from the book along the perforated lines. Cut out the file-folder label and pocket on page 37. Glue the label onto the file-folder tab. Tape the sides and bottom of the pocket to the front of the folder.

2 Cut out the directions, answer key, and game cards on pages 39 and 41. When the game is not in use, store these items in the pocket on the front of the folder.

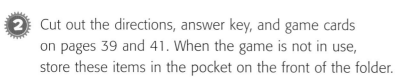

3 Cut out the two game boards on pages 43 and 45 and glue them to the inside of the folder.

4 Cut out and assemble the game cube and game markers on page 47.

EXTENDING THE GAME

Challenge children to play the game by taking away time. To prepare, make a copy of the game board. Mask "Add" on the spaces and write in "Take away." Then make two copies of the game board. Invite two children to play the game, this time taking away 10 minutes, 30 minutes, or one hour from the time on the game cards.

Run Up the Clock

GET READY TO PLAY

- Each player chooses a game board and game marker.
- Place your marker on Start on your game board.
- Shuffle the cards. Stack them facedown.

TO PLAY

1 Roll the game cube. Move that number of spaces. If the cube lands on the 🐱, your turn ends.

2 Did you land on a blank space? If so, your turn ends.

3 Did you land on a space with directions? If so, take the top card on the stack. Read the time. Then add the amount of time on the space. Tell the new time.

4 After each turn, check the answer key. Is your answer correct? If not, move your marker back.

5 Keep taking turns. The first player to reach Finish wins the game.

PLAYING TIP

At the end of each turn, players put their card at the bottom of the stack.

Run Up the Clock

ANSWER KEY

	add 10 minutes	add 30 minutes	add 1 hour		add 10 minutes	add 30 minutes	add 1 hour
1:10	1:20	1:40	2:10	**6:30**	6:40	7:00	7:30
1:30	1:40	2:00	2:30	**7:00**	7:10	7:30	8:00
2:10	2:20	2:40	3:10	**7:30**	7:40	8:00	8:30
2:20	2:30	2:50	3:20	**8:10**	8:20	8:40	9:10
3:00	3:10	3:30	4:00	**8:40**	8:50	9:10	9:40
4:00	4:10	4:30	5:00	**9:00**	9:10	9:30	10:00
4:20	4:30	4:50	5:20	**9:20**	9:30	9:50	10:20
5:10	5:20	5:40	6:10	**10:50**	11:00	11:20	11:50
5:40	5:50	6:10	6:40	**11:30**	11:40	12:00	12:30
6:20	6:30	6:50	7:20	**12:40**	12:50	1:10	1:40

1:10	1:30	2:10	2:20
3:00	4:00	4:20	5:10
5:40	6:20	6:30	7:00
7:30	8:10	8:40	9:00
9:20	10:50	11:30	12:40

Add 30 minutes.	Add 1 hour.		Add 30 minutes.	Add 10 minutes.	FINISH

Add 10 minutes.	Add 1 hour.				

	Add 30 minutes.	Add 1 hour.		Add 10 minutes.	

					Add 30 minutes.

				Add 30 minutes.	Add 1 hour.

START	Add 1 hour.	Add 10 minutes.		Add 10 minutes.	

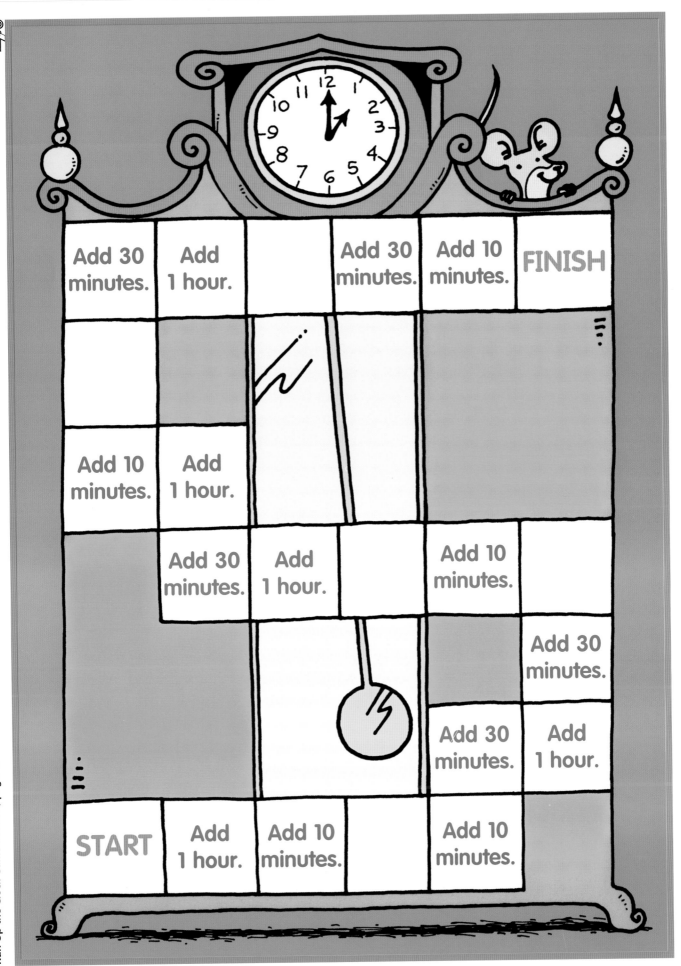

Add 30 minutes.

Add 1 hour.

Add 30 minutes.

Add 10 minutes.

FINISH

Add 10 minutes.

Add 1 hour.

Add 30 minutes.

Add 1 hour.

Add 10 minutes.

Add 30 minutes.

Add 30 minutes.

Add 1 hour.

START

Add 1 hour.

Add 10 minutes.

Add 10 minutes.

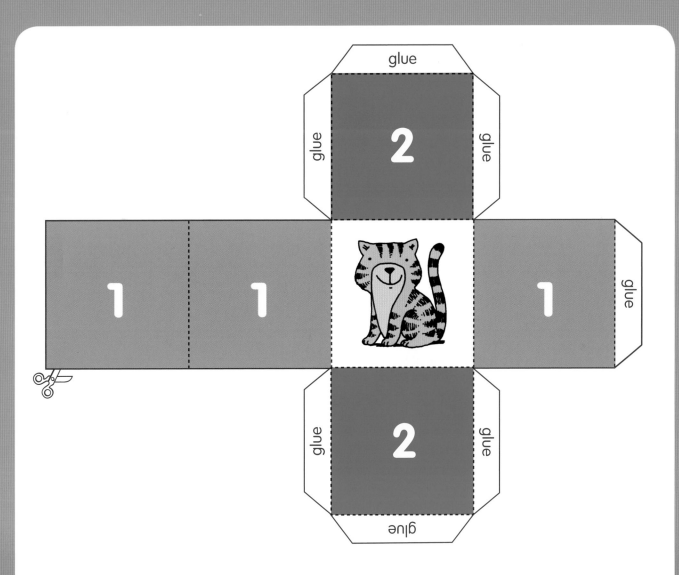

Fold the tabs on the game markers
so they stand up.

Fold here.

Fold here.

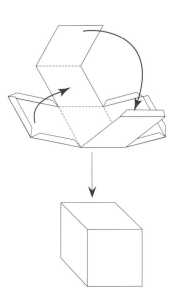

Assemble the cube by folding as shown. Glue closed.

Run Up the Clock Game Cube and Game Markers

Perfect Pooch Academy

SKILL

This game gives children practice in matching digital times to time phrases.

INTRODUCTION

Display a set of three game cards. Write a time phrase on the chalk- or whiteboard that matches the time on one of the cards. Spell out the phrase to match the way the time would be read (for example, write "two-thirty" for 2:30). Then ask children to read the time on each card to find the one that matches the time phrase on the board. Invite a volunteer to point out the correct card. Repeat the activity, changing the game cards and writing a different time phrase each time. Then show children the game boards. Explain that each game board represents a pooch's schedule.

ASSEMBLING THE GAME

1. Remove pages 51–59 from the book along the perforated lines. Cut out the file-folder label and pocket on page 51. Glue the label onto the file-folder tab. Tape the sides and bottom of the pocket to the front of the folder.

2. Cut out the directions, answer key, and game cards on pages 53 and 55. When the game is not in use, store these items in the pocket on the front of the folder.

3. Cut out the two game boards on pages 57 and 59 and glue them to the inside of the folder.

EXTENDING THE GAME

Stamp analog clock faces on 24 plain index cards. Draw hands on each clock to match a time shown on the game boards. Then invite children to play the game using the analog clock cards. They can cover the boxes on their game boards with large buttons, round counters, or paper markers that have been cut to fit the size of the boxes.

Perfect Pooch Academy

Perfect Pooch Academy

GET READY TO PLAY

- Each player chooses a game board.
- Shuffle the cards. Stack them facedown.

TO PLAY

1 Take the card from the top of the stack.
Read the time on the card.
Check to see if a time phrase on your schedule
matches that time. Did you find a match?

- If so, put the card on the match.
- If not, put the card at the bottom of the stack

2 After each turn, check the answer key. Is your answer correct?
If not, put the card at the bottom of the stack.

3 Keep taking turns. Try to cover all of your boxes.
The first player to do this wins the game.

Perfect Pooch Academy

ANSWER KEY

Game Board 1		Game Board 2	
8:30	12:30	8:30	12:00
8:45	1:15	8:45	12:15
9:15	1:30	9:30	1:00
9:45	2:15	9:45	2:15
10:30	2:45	10:30	2:45
12:00	3:30	11:30	3:30

8:30	8:30	8:45	8:45
9:15	9:30	9:45	9:45
10:30	10:30	11:30	12:00
12:00	12:15	12:30	1:00
1:15	1:30	2:15	2:15
2:45	2:45	3:30	3:30

Perfect Pooch Academy

eight-thirty

twelve-thirty

eight-forty-five

one-fifteen

nine-fifteen

one-thirty

nine-forty-five

two-fifteen

ten-thirty

two-forty-five

twelve o'clock

three-thirty

Perfect Pooch Academy

eight-thirty

twelve o'clock

eight-forty-five

twelve-fifteen

nine-thirty

one o'clock

nine-forty-five

two-fifteen

ten-thirty

two-forty-five

eleven-thirty

three-thirty

Time Tiger

PLAYERS: 2

SKILL

This game gives children practice in identifying different units of time.

INTRODUCTION

Create a five-column chart with the headings "Day of Week," "Month of Year," "Season of Year," "Time of Day," and "Time on Clock." Write each word from the game boards on separate index cards, one card for each word. Then show one card at a time to children and read it aloud. Ask them to tell which column heading best describes the category to which that unit of time belongs. Invite a volunteer to attach the card to that column using removable adhesive. After placing all of the cards on the chart, review the units of time that belong to each category.

ASSEMBLING THE GAME

1. Remove pages 63–73 from the book along the perforated lines. Cut out the file-folder label and pocket on page 63. Glue the label onto the file-folder tab. Tape the sides and bottom of the pocket to the front of the folder.

2. Cut out the directions, answer key, and game markers on pages 65 and 67. When the game is not in use, store these items in the pocket on the front of the folder.

3. Cut out the two game boards on pages 69 and 71 and glue them to the inside of the folder.

4. Cut out and assemble the game spinner on page 73.

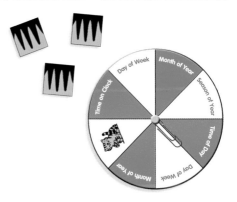

EXTENDING THE GAME

Label index cards with the months, the seasons, and the days of the week. Distribute one card to each child. Have children curl up on the floor and pretend to be sleeping tigers. Explain that you will call out a specific month, season, or day. If a tiger has that word card, he or she "wakes" up, "roars" out the word, and tells what category it belongs to.

Time Tiger

GET READY TO PLAY

- Each player chooses a game board and 16 game markers.

TO PLAY

1 Spin the spinner. Does it land on the 🐱? If so, take a free turn!
Read the word in any box on your game board.
Then place a on the box. Take another turn.

2 Read the phrase on the spinner.
Check the boxes on your game board.
Does a unit of time match that phrase?

- If so, read the unit of time. Then place a on that box.

- If not, your turn ends.

3 After each turn, check the answer key. Is your answer correct?
If not, take the back.

4 Keep taking turns. Try to cover four boxes in a row—going across,
down, or diagonally. The first player to do this wins the game.

PLAYING TIP

Play the game another way: Try to cover all of the boxes on your game board.
The first player to do this wins the game.

Time Tiger

ANSWER KEY

Day of Week	Month of Year		Time of Day
Sunday	January	September	morning
Monday	February	October	afternoon
Tuesday	March	November	night
Wednesday	April	December	
Thursday	May	**Season of Year**	**Time on Clock**
Friday	June	Fall	hour
Saturday	July	Winter	half hour
	August	Spring	minute
		Summer	second

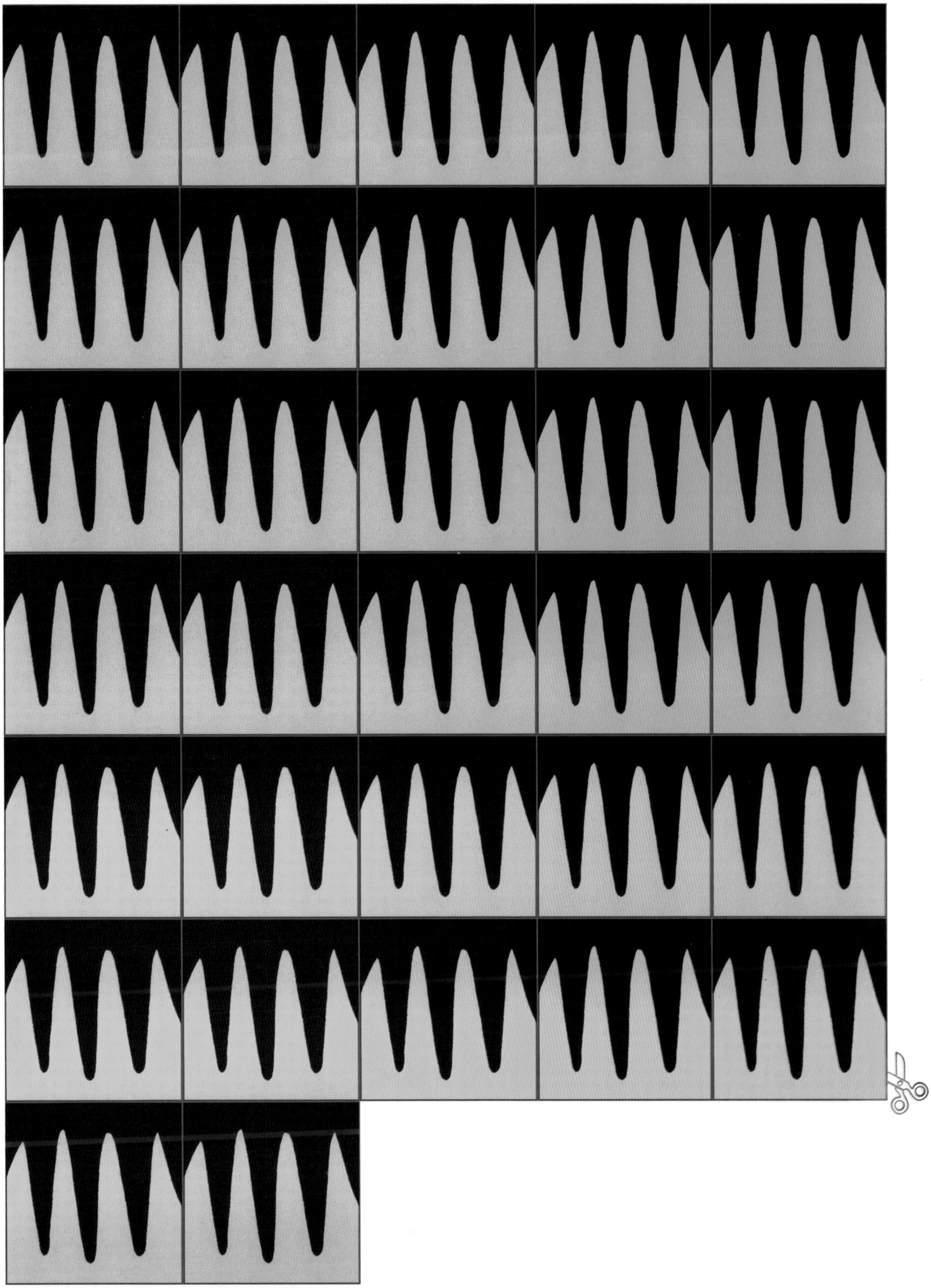

Friday	Winter	July	hour
Sunday	January	afternoon	Monday
December	Fall	minute	April
May	Wednesday	October	night

Spring	February	second	afternoon
June	Thursday	September	half hour
November	morning	March	Saturday
Tuesday	August	Wednesday	Summer

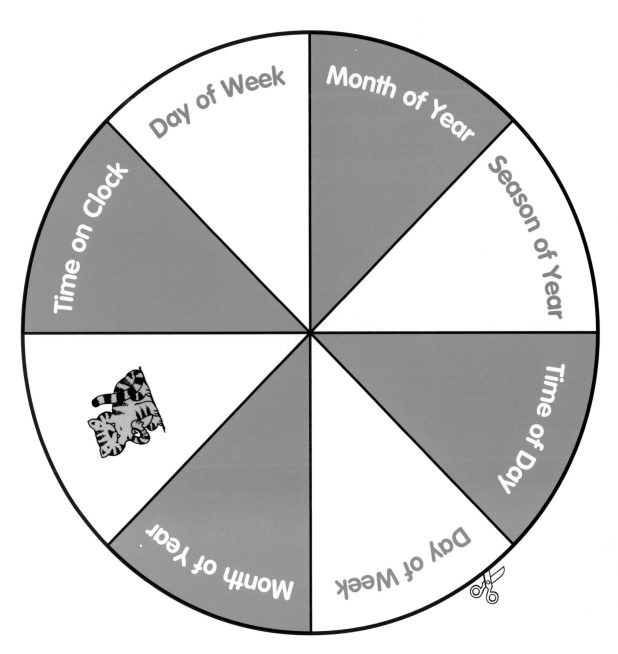

Day of Week

Month of Year

Time on Clock

Season of Year

Time of Day

Month of Year

Day of Week

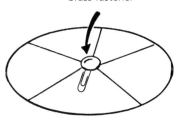

brass fastener

Assemble the spinner using a paper clip and brass fastener as shown. Make sure the paper clip spins easily.

Money Merry-Go-Round

PLAYERS: 2

SKILL

This game gives children practice in matching individual coins to their value.

INTRODUCTION

Write the following money amounts on the headings of a five-column chart: 1¢, 5¢, 10¢, 25¢, and 50¢. Then show one game card at a time to children. Ask them to tell the value of the coin on the card. Invite a volunteer to find the column labeled with that amount and then place the card in the column using removable adhesive. After placing all of the game cards on the chart, have children compare the different coins and their values.

ASSEMBLING THE GAME

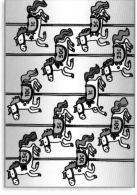

1. Remove pages 77–87 from the book along the perforated lines. Cut out the file-folder label and pocket on page 77. Glue the label onto the file-folder tab. Tape the sides and bottom of the pocket to the front of the folder.

2. Cut out the directions, answer key, and game cards on pages 79 and 81. When the game is not in use, store these items in the pocket on the front of the folder.

3. Cut out the two game boards on pages 83 and 85 and glue them to the inside of the folder.

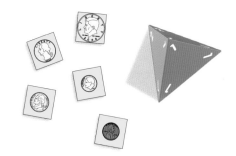

4. Cut out and assemble the number pyramid on page 87.

EXTENDING THE GAME

Copy and laminate the game cards. Attach magnetic tape to the back of each one. Put the cards in a center along with a write-on magnet board, wipe-off pen, and paper towels. To use, children pick two cards and attach them to the magnet board, leaving a space between them. Then they name the coin on each card, compare the value of the two coins, and write <, >, or = in the space between the cards to create a number sentence.

Money Merry-Go-Round

PLAYERS: 2

GET READY TO PLAY

- Each player chooses a game board.
- Shuffle the cards. Stack them facedown.

TO PLAY

1 Roll the game cube. Take that number of cards.

2 Name the coin on each card and tell its value.
Is that amount on one of your horses?
- If so, place the card on that horse.
- If not, place the card at the bottom of the stack.

3 After each turn, check the answer key. Is each answer correct?
If not, put that card at the bottom of the stack.

4 Keep taking turns. Try to cover all of your horses.
The first player to do this wins the game.

Money Merry-Go-Round

ANSWER KEY

 1¢

 25¢

 5¢

 50¢

 10¢

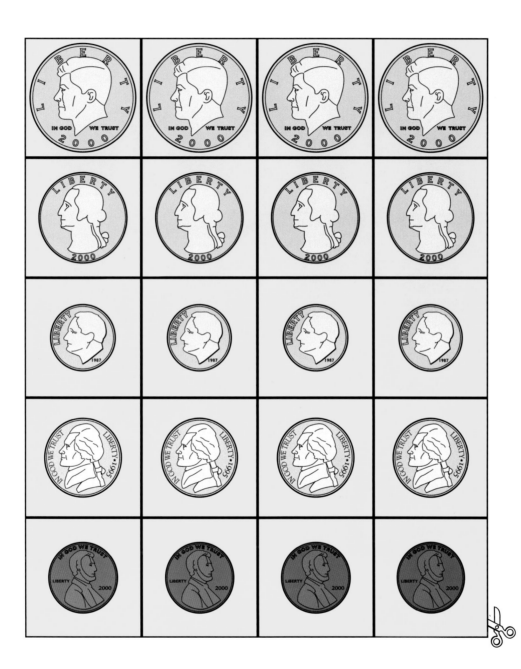

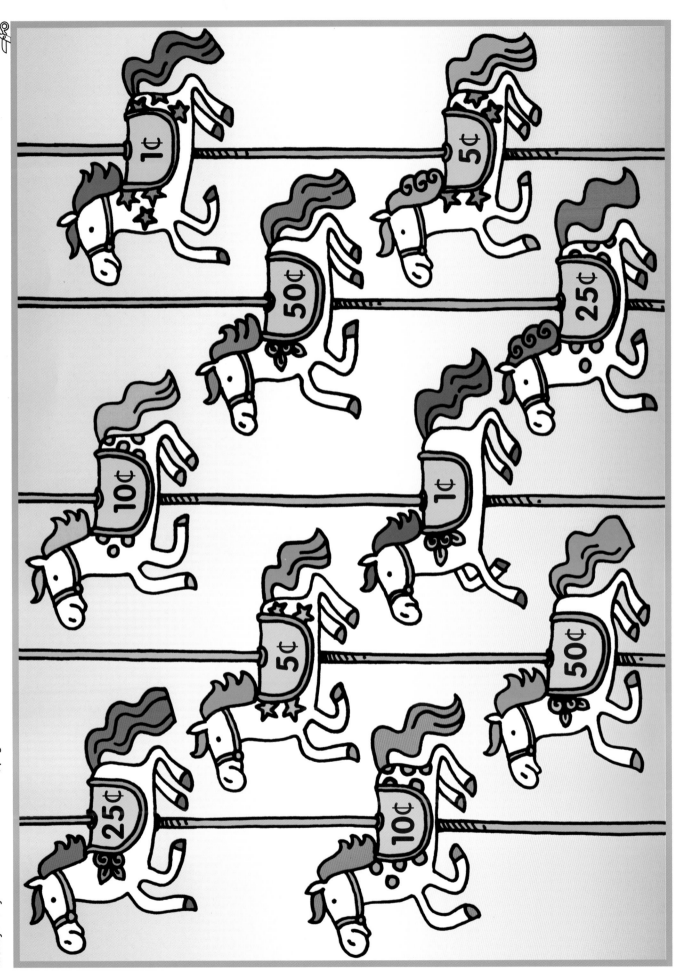

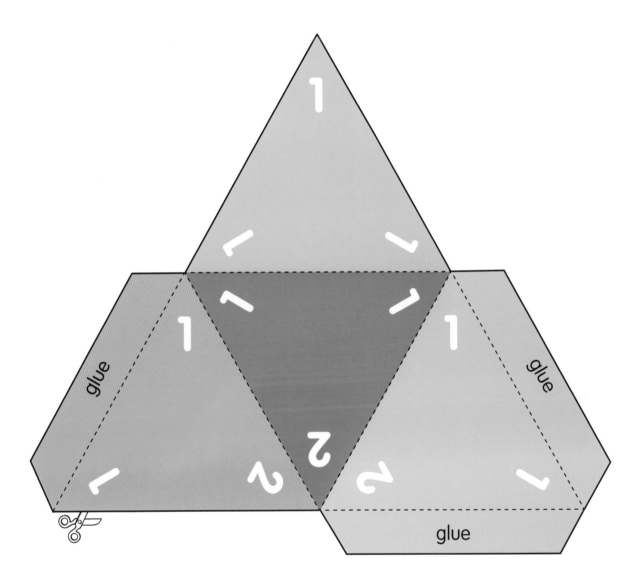

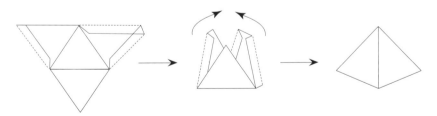

Assemble the pyramid by folding as shown. Glue closed.

Coin Collectors

SKILL

This game gives children practice in adding the value of a penny, nickel, dime, or quarter to different money amounts.

INTRODUCTION

Hold up a plastic penny and have children tell its value. Then show one game card at a time to children. Ask them to find the value of the coin combination on the card. Next, have them add the value of the penny to the value of the coins. What's the new value? Continue, alternating the use of a penny, nickel, dime, and quarter, and having children add the value of that coin to the value of the coins on a card.

ASSEMBLING THE GAME

1 Remove pages 91–101 from the book along the perforated lines. Cut out the file-folder label and pocket on page 91. Glue the label onto the file-folder tab. Tape the sides and bottom of the pocket to the front of the folder.

2 Cut out the directions, answer key, and game cards on pages 93 and 95. When the game is not in use, store these items in the pocket on the front of the folder.

3 Cut out the two sides of the game board on pages 97 and 99 and glue them to the inside of the folder.

4 Cut out and assemble the game cube and game markers on page 101.

EXTENDING THE GAME

Make 12 copies of the game markers. Laminate and cut out each one. Then use a wipe-off pen to write a money amount from 1¢ to 50¢ on the back of each marker. Stand the markers up in a center and add a set of plastic coins containing pennies, nickels, dimes, and quarters. Ask children to choose a marker and a coin. Have them add the value of the coin to the amount on the back of the marker and tell the new amount.

Coin Collectors

GET READY TO PLAY

- Each player places a game marker on any ▇ space on the game board.
- Shuffle the game cards. Stack them facedown.

TO PLAY

1 Roll the game cube. Move that number of spaces.
If you land on a coin, take a card from the top of the stack.

2 Find the value of the coin(s) on the card. Tell the amount.
Then add the value of the coin on the space.
What is the new amount? Tell the other players your answer.

3 After each turn, check the answer key. Is your answer correct?
- If so, keep the card.
- If not, put the card at the bottom of the stack.

4 Keep taking turns until all the cards have been used.
Players then count their cards.
The player with the most cards wins the game.

PLAYING TIPS

- Players may land on and share the same space.
- Players may move around the game board as many times as needed.

Coin Collectors

ANSWER KEY

🪙	2¢	4¢	6¢	11¢	16¢	11¢	14¢	16¢	21¢	26¢
🪙	6¢	8¢	10¢	15¢	20¢	15¢	18¢	20¢	25¢	30¢
🪙	11¢	13¢	15¢	20¢	25¢	20¢	23¢	25¢	30¢	35¢
🪙	26¢	28¢	30¢	35¢	40¢	35¢	38¢	40¢	45¢	50¢

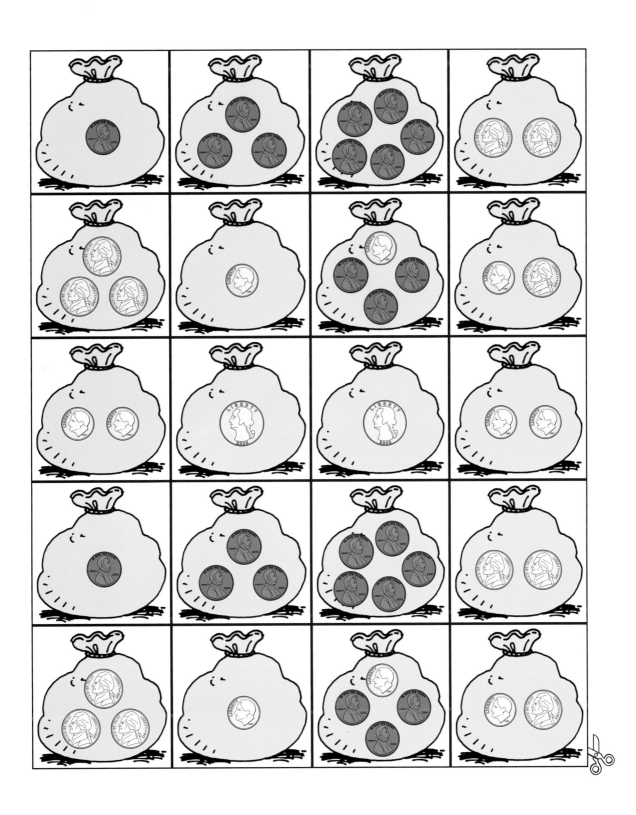

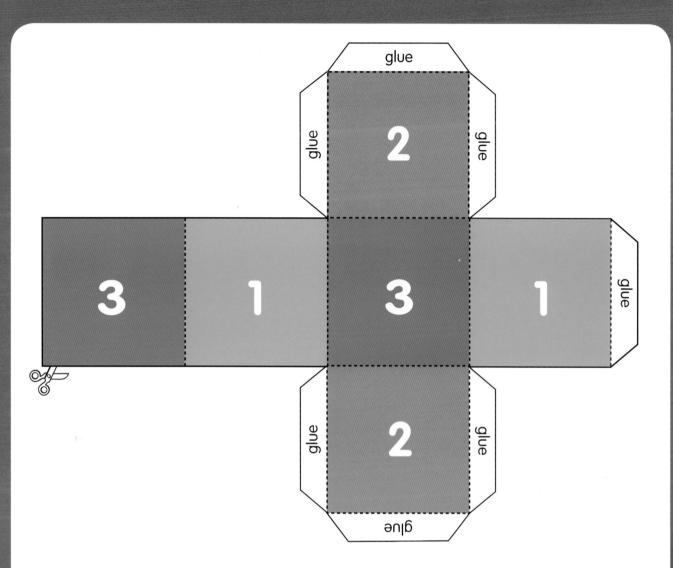

glue

glue 2 glue

3 1 3 1 glue

glue 2 glue

glue

Fold the tabs on the game markers
so they stand up.

Fold here. Fold here. Fold here.

Assemble the cube by folding as shown. Glue closed.

Build the Bank

SKILL This game gives children practice in finding the value of coin combinations to 99¢.

INTRODUCTION

Show children one game card at a time and ask them to find the value of the coin combination. Invite volunteers to share their answers. Then review the value of each coin. Ask children to tell how they arrived at the total value of the coins. If desired, provide plastic or real coins for children to use. They might count out the coins to demonstrate how they reached their answer. Finally, write the correct answer for each combination on the chalk- or whiteboard.

ASSEMBLING THE GAME

1 Remove pages 105–115 from the book along the perforated lines. Cut out the file-folder label and pocket on page 105. Glue the label onto the file-folder tab. Tape the sides and bottom of the pocket to the front of the folder.

2 Cut out the directions, answer key, and game cards on pages 107, 109, and 111. When the game is not in use, store these items in the pocket on the front of the folder.

3 Cut out the two game boards on pages 113 and 115 and glue them to the inside of the folder.

Build the Bank

60¢	11¢	53¢	75¢
8¢	25¢	96¢	30¢
41¢	16¢	3¢	22¢
82¢	37¢	78¢	15¢

Build the Bank

28¢	40¢	12¢	87¢
52¢	17¢	91¢	45¢
9¢	33¢	26¢	77¢
20¢	63¢	35¢	4¢

EXTENDING THE GAME

Place the game cards and a set of plastic coins in your math center. Pair up children. Invite the partners to take turns picking a card and finding the corresponding plastic coins. Ask them to find the value of their coin combination and then have their partner check their work.

Build the Bank

GET READY TO PLAY

- Each player chooses a game board.
- Shuffle the cards. Stack them facedown.

TO PLAY

1 Take a card from the top of the stack.
Find the value of the coins on the card.
Check your game board for that amount.

2 Did you find a match?
- If so, place the card on the matching box.
- If not, put the card at the bottom of the stack.

3 After each turn, check the answer key. Is your answer correct?
If not, put the card at the bottom of the stack.

4 Keep taking turns. Try to cover all of your boxes.
The first player to do this wins the game.

Build the Bank

ANSWER KEY

Game Board 1

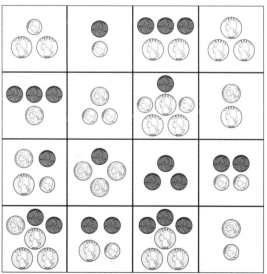

Game Board 2

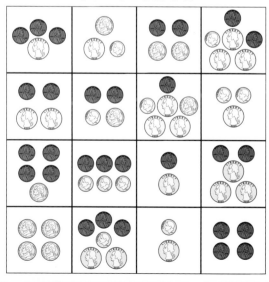

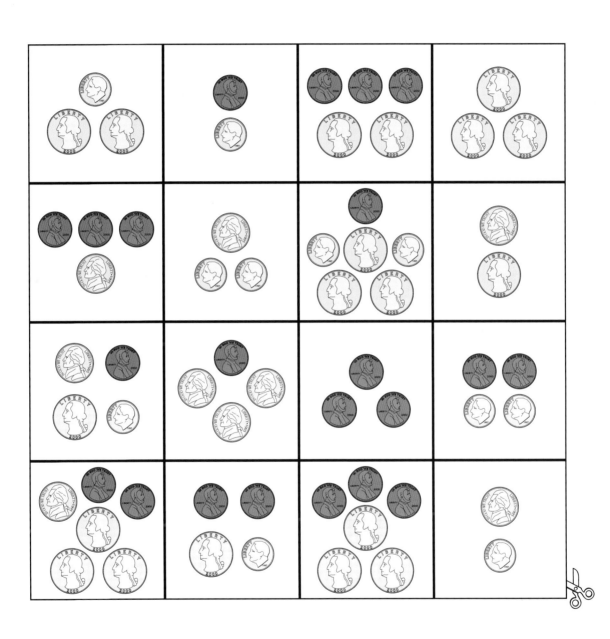

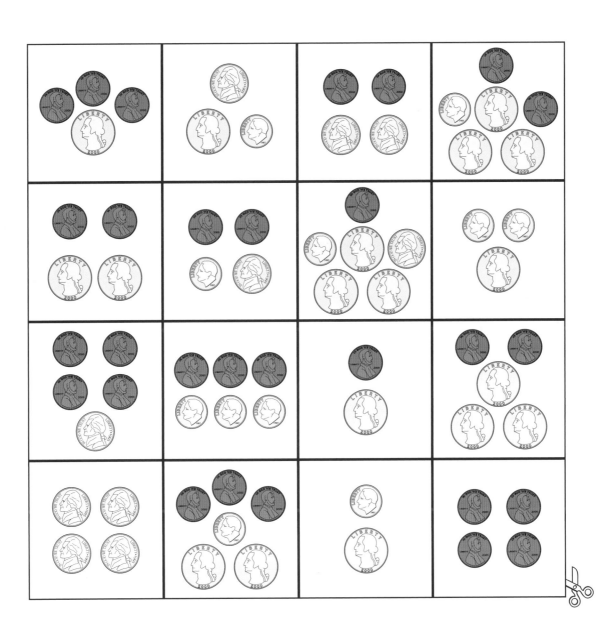

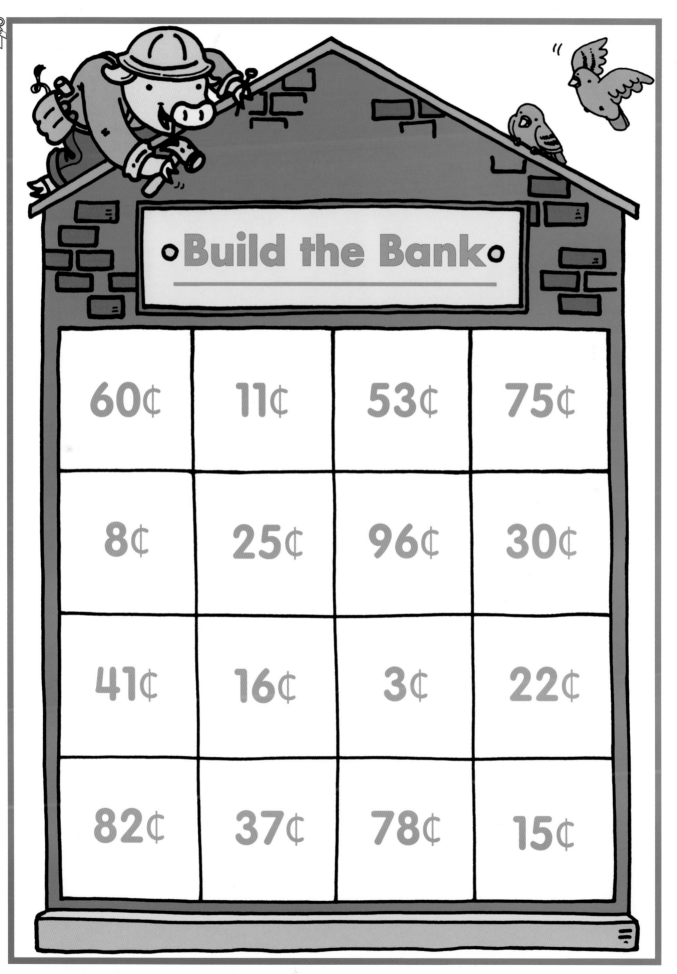

Build the Bank

60¢	11¢	53¢	75¢
8¢	25¢	96¢	30¢
41¢	16¢	3¢	22¢
82¢	37¢	78¢	15¢

Build the Bank

28¢	40¢	12¢	87¢
52¢	17¢	91¢	45¢
9¢	33¢	26¢	77¢
20¢	63¢	35¢	4¢

Koala's Coins

PLAYERS: 2

 SKILL

This game gives children practice in sorting coin combinations by their value.

INTRODUCTION

Write the following on the headings of a four-column chart: 15¢ or less, 16¢ to 30¢, 31¢ to 50¢, and 51¢ or more. Then show one game card at a time to children. Have them find the value of the coins on the card and then find the column in which that value fits. Invite a volunteer to attach the card to the chart using removable adhesive. Then discuss the value and why it fits in the money range shown for that column. Repeat for each game card.

ASSEMBLING THE GAME

1. Remove pages 119–129 from the book along the perforated lines. Cut out the file-folder label and pocket on page 119. Glue the label onto the file-folder tab. Tape the sides and bottom of the pocket to the front of the folder.

 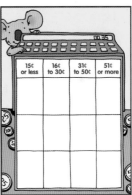

2. Cut out the directions, answer key, and game cards on pages 121 and 123. When the game is not in use, store these items in the pocket on the front of the folder.

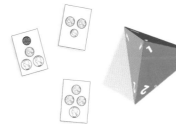

3. Cut out the two game boards on pages 125 and 127 and glue them to the inside of the folder.

4. Cut out and assemble the number pyramid on page 129.

EXTENDING THE GAME

Cut out two large circles from construction paper. Label one circle "40¢ or less" and the other "41¢ or more." Place the game cards in a paper bag. Then have children draw one card at a time, find the value of the coins on the card, and place it on the appropriate circle. For later rounds, change the money amounts on the circles.

Koala's Coins

GET READY TO PLAY

- Each player chooses a game board.
- Shuffle the cards. Stack them facedown.

TO PLAY

1. Roll the number pyramid. Take that number of cards.

2. Find the value of the coins on each card.
   Look at the money ranges at the top of your game board.
   In which range does the value of your coins fit?

3. Check the boxes in that column. Is there an empty box?
   - If so, put the card on an empty box.
   - If not, put the card at the bottom of the stack.

4. After each turn, check the answer key. Is each answer correct?
   If not, put that card at the bottom of the stack.

5. Keep taking turns. Try to fill all of your boxes.
   The first player to do this wins the game.

Koala's Coins

ANSWER KEY

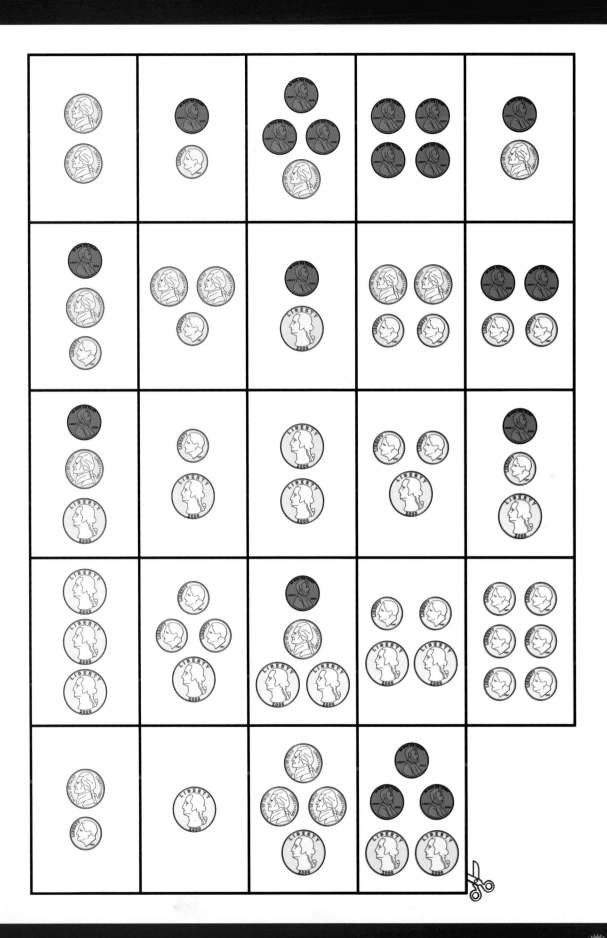

00.35

15¢ or less	16¢ to 30¢	31¢ to 50¢	51¢ or more

00.35

15¢ or less	16¢ to 30¢	31¢ to 50¢	51¢ or more

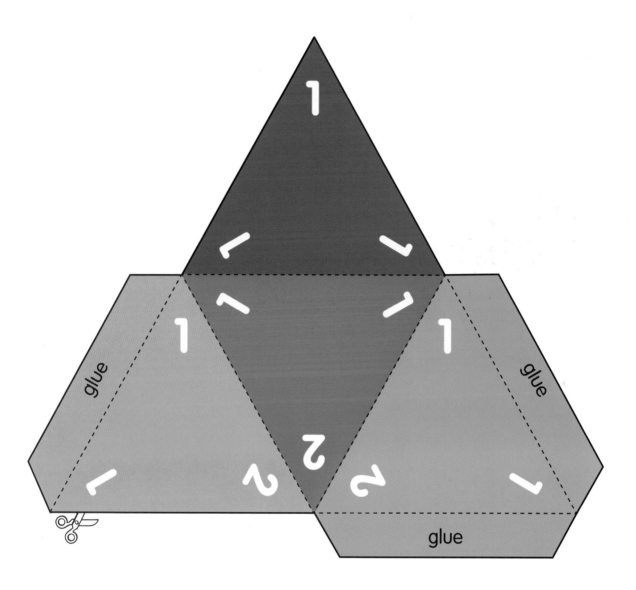

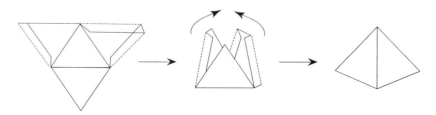

Assemble the pyramid by folding as shown. Glue closed.

Shopping Spree

SKILL

This game gives children practice in finding the value of money combinations from $1.00 to $2.00.

INTRODUCTION

Write each of the following money amounts on separate sticky notes: $1.00, $1.05, $1.10, $1.15, $1.20, $1.25, $1.30, $1.40, $1.50, $1.75, and $2.00. Then attach three notes to the chalk- or whiteboard. Show children a game card that has a combination of money that matches one of the amounts on the displayed sticky notes. Ask them to find the value of the money and then identify the sticky note labeled with that amount. Repeat, each time using different sets of sticky notes and a different game card.

ASSEMBLING THE GAME

1. Remove pages 133–143 from the book along the perforated lines. Cut out the file-folder label and pocket on page 133. Glue the label onto the file-folder tab. Tape the sides and bottom of the pocket to the front of the folder.

2. Cut out the directions, answer key, and game cards on pages 135 and 137. When the game is not in use, store these items in the pocket on the front of the folder.

3. Cut out the two sides of the game board on pages 139 and 141 and glue them to the inside of the folder.

4. Cut out and assemble the game cube and game markers on page 143.

EXTENDING THE GAME

Copy the game boards and cut out the pictures of the store items, leaving off the tags. Glue each picture to a separate index card. Then write a price on each card. Place the cards in a center with a set of play money, including paper bills and coins. To use, children pick a card, read the price of the pictured item, and count out the amount of money needed to "buy" the item. Have children work in pairs, taking turns buying items and checking each other's work.

Shopping Spree

GET READY TO PLAY

- Each player places a game marker on any ■ space on the game board.
- Shuffle the game cards. Deal five cards to each player. Stack the rest facedown.

TO PLAY

1. Roll the game cube. Move that number of spaces.

2. Does your space have a picture on it? If so, read the price of that item. Do you have a card with that amount of money on it?
   - If so, set the card aside.
   - If not, take the card from the top of the stack. Is the new card a match? If so, set it aside. If not, your turn ends.

3. After each turn, check the answer key. Is your answer correct? If not, take the card back.

4. Keep taking turns. Try to get rid of all of your cards. The first player to do this wins the game.

PLAYING TIPS

- Players may land on and share the same space.
- Players may move around the game board as many times as needed.
- When no cards are left in the stack, players continue using the cards in their hands.

Shopping Spree

ANSWER KEY

$1.00:			**$1.20:**			**$1.50:**	
$1.05:			**$1.25:**			**$1.75:**	
$1.10:			**$1.30:**			**$2.00:**	
$1.15:			**$1.40:**				

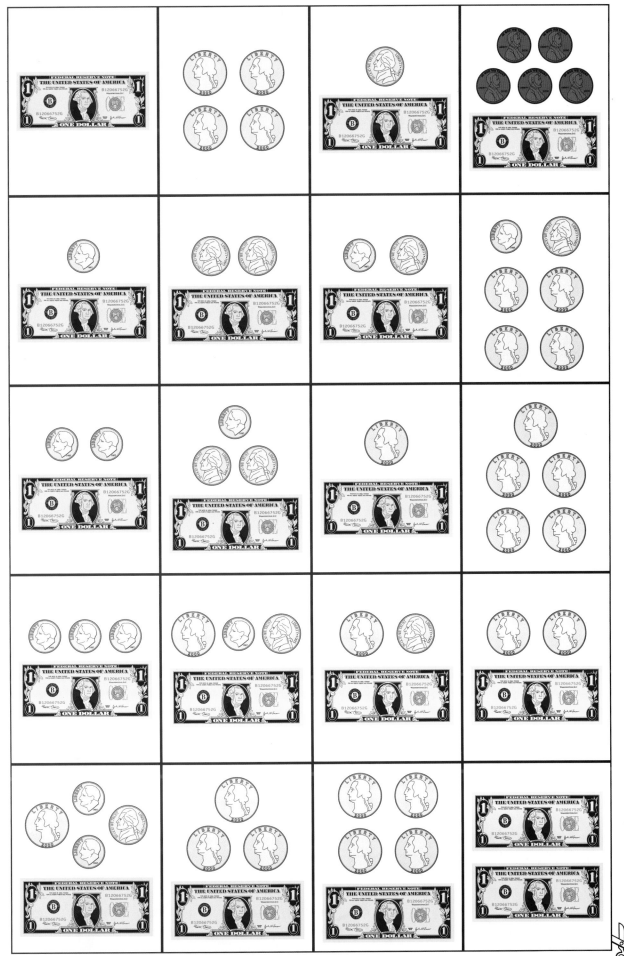

$2.00

$1.20

$1.25

$1.40

$1.10

$1.30

$1.15

$1.50

$1.05

$1.00

SPACE

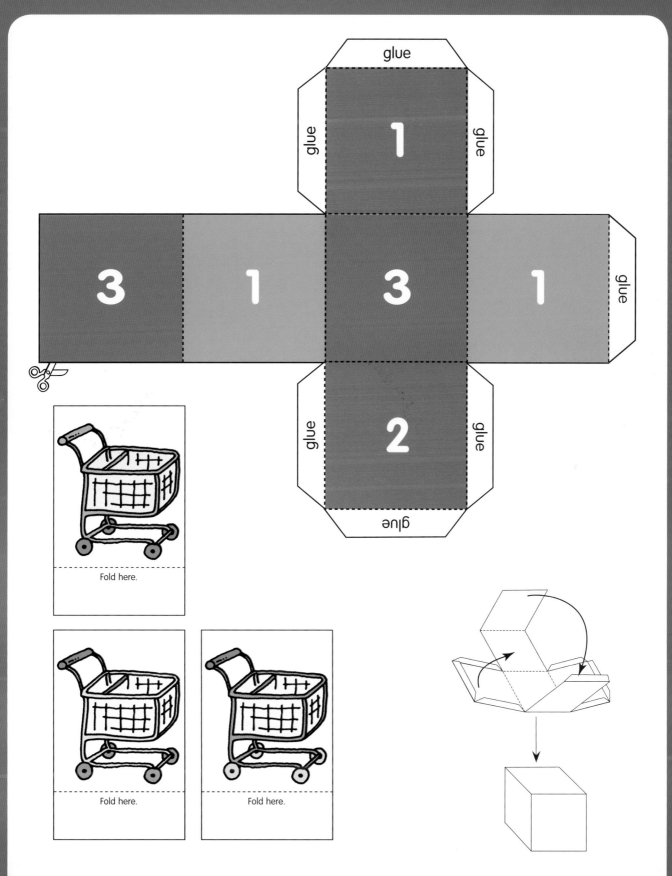

Assemble the cube by folding as shown. Glue closed.